BOXING
FOR BEGINNERS

BOXING
FOR BEGINNERS
AL BERNSTEIN

 Contemporary Books, Inc.
Chicago

Library of Congress Cataloging in Publication Data

Bernstein, Al.
  Boxing for beginners.

  Includes index.
  1. Boxing.   I. Title.
GV1133.B44   1978   796.8'3   77-23690
ISBN 0-8092-7758-1
ISBN 0-8092-7757-3 pbk.

Thanks to the Chicago Park District for its cooperation. With the exception of photographs of Ken Norton, all photographs are of Clarendon Park boxing team members in Chicago.

All photographs of Ken Norton were provided by Robert Goodman.

Special thanks go to David Burns, Robert Feder, and Louis Lang.

Photos by Barbara Bergwerf.

Published by Contemporary Books, Inc.
180 North Michigan Avenue, Chicago, Illinois 60601
Manufactured in the United States of America
Library of Congress Catalog Card Number: 77-23690
International Standard Book Number: 0-8092-7758-1 (cloth)
                                     0-8092-7757-3 (paper)

Published simultaneously in Canada by
Beaverbooks
953 Dillingham Road
Pickering, Ontario L1W 1Z7
Canada

Contents

Introduction
by Ken Norton

Today people in the street call me "Champ." The sportswriters are calling me the "Uncrowned Heavyweight Champion." That's all very flattering, and I do enjoy every bit of it. Few people, however, truly realize the kind of life you have to lead to be a top professional boxer.

It is a very hard and lonely life with long periods of sacrifice and hard work. In preparation for a major fight, I spend six to eight weeks in camp training for that one evening. There are many long periods away from my family. My training team becomes my family in camp. We all have to endure the same hardships, working for one common goal—victory.

Not all of you will want to become professional boxers. I'm sure that very few of you who read this book have that in mind to begin with. Very few can really make it to the top.

But then again, you never know. My good friend Joe Frazier walked into the gym in Philadelphia one afternoon because he wanted to lose some weight and went on to become the Heavyweight Champion of the World.

I've played football, basketball, baseball, and run the hurdles in track and thrown the discus in field events. It always came pretty easy for me. I was a natural athlete who was blessed with good reflexes and a strong, healthy body.

I didn't start boxing until I was 22 years old. It was football and track for me with a scholarship in college, and I didn't give boxing a thought until I was in the U. S. Marine Corps. I wish that boxing came as easily as the other sports but it was much tougher. I felt a little awkward for a long time.

It would have helped a great deal if there had been a book to refer to and study like *Boxing for Beginners*. Al Bernstein, who wrote this book, has a fine knowledge of boxing and has put his ideas and experiences into an easy to study and read format.

I owe a great deal to boxing. There are a great many wonderful people in boxing who are always ready to help less fortunate people by giving of themselves.

The most important thing to remember for you youngsters out there with an interest in sports or boxing in particular is to get your education. You can always go to the gym four or five days a week without neglecting your studies. It's important in boxing to have a healthy mind as well as a healthy body. Today's boxers are intelligent, thinking athletes. Fewer boxers are hurt seriously each year than athletes in any of the other major contact sports. And don't forget, there are probably more boxers in this world than any other kind of athlete.

Some of you might just want to get into shape and learn how to defend yourselves. There are many fine amateur programs in most states. Just about every major city has boxing programs for youngsters.

I like the individual effort in boxing and also the contact. Once you climb up those four steps into the ring, it is just you against another man with the same basic physical equipment.

The little man also has equal opportunity in boxing that he often doesn't have in other sports. In boxing, you fight men within your weight division. You will never be in against a man twice your size, unless you're a heavyweight and you happen to be fighting King Kong. The same cannot be said of other contact sports, where size is very important.

Boxing is a great character builder. Although not all of you will pursue the instructions in this book on to professional boxing, everyone who reads it and applies it will certainly get something out of it.

1

The Start-Up

The sport of boxing may well be in the midst of its most popular period since the mid-1950s. Interest in the "sweet science" has increased on both amateur and professional levels, both in the United States and in other parts of the world.

Boxing, like most other sports, has suffered through some bleak periods and has enjoyed some boom periods. But whatever its temporary fortunes may have been, the sport has always remained. That is because there always have been young men eager to meet the ultimate challenge in skill, strength, and cunning that boxing provides. The idea of beating another man on the most basic terms (with rules and regulations as a safeguard) is what all sport is built on, and no sport provides that opportunity better than boxing does.

Boxing is a complex and fascinating sport for observer and participant, and especially for a participant.

Because of the increased interest in the sport, many more young men are becoming boxers than in the 1960s. In any sport the beginning period can determine whether you stay with it and whether you ever become proficient. With boxing, this is especially true.

The best way to learn to box is to acquaint yourself with the fundamentals, get into good condition, and then join a recognized boxing club or class. These clubs and classes can be found at your local park district, at B'nai Brith or Catholic Youth organizations, or at a school in your area.

You cannot learn to box entirely on your own. This book can provide the fundamentals and help you in the beginning period, but at some point you will need a trainer or coach to work with you on a regular basis.

Before you are ready to begin boxing, you must understand a few things about the preparation process.

Time Requirement

Boxing is unlike other sports in that the time requirement is generally more for a boxer than other athletes. Boxing, even on an amateur level, requires a large commitment in your lifestyle if you want to excel.

Obviously most amateur boxers cannot devote full time to the sport. They generally have work or school commitments during the day. Because of that, boxing training usually is done at training centers on weeknights and weekends. To become at all proficient in the sport, expect to spend two or three nights a week at a training center and perhaps a weekend day there also.

Depending on the length of the workouts at your training center and your zeal for the sport, you may find some lighter workouts at home helpful too. These lighter workouts help keep your muscles toned for the heavier training at the gym.

As you read the next few chapters and as you get into boxing training at your club, you will find that the idea of extensive training is not as brutal as it may sound at first. The training and learning period for a beginning boxer is probably the most rewarding part of boxing. The realization at some point that you have turned your body into an effective fighting machine should make you want to train more.

The best outfit for a boxer to work out in is a complete sweatsuit like this one. You should purchase one before starting your boxing training.

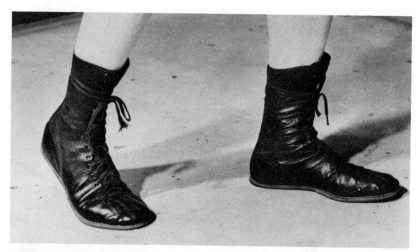

The best footwear for workouts as well as matches is a pair of hightop boxing shoes like these. Gym shoes may do for a while, but as you continue your boxing training, regulation boxing shoes will be necessary.

These gloves are used for work on the speed bag and heavy bag in training. Some boxing centers provide these gloves, but others do not.

Equipment

Much of the major equipment needs of a boxer are provided for at the training center where he trains. But you will need to obtain several items yourself when you begin to box.

First, you will need a workout outfit. This should include a sweat suit, shorts, and a pair of boxing shoes.

The sweat suit is the best garb for working out because it helps you sweat off any unwanted weight. Many fighters are tempted to work out in just gym shorts or boxing trunks. For a boxer with a good build, it may be an ego boost, but it won't help any in training.

High-top boxing shoes are a good investment for a beginning boxer. For a time, you may be able to get by wearing gym shoes to a workout, but before too long, you will need boxing shoes. Boxing shoes are also better protection against ankle injuries.

You will need a rubber or plastic mouthpiece, which all boxers use in sparring and during fights to protect their teeth and tongue from injuries. Mouthpieces are available in various kinds, ranging from a simple one that fits everyone to specially fitted types that dentists provide. The basic mouthpiece is sufficient for beginning boxers.

A pair of speed gloves also is essential. These gloves are used while working on the speed bag and heavy bag in training. Normally they are not provided by boxing clubs.

Hand-wrappings usually are not provided by boxing centers either, and all boxers need these wrappings for sparring and for matches. Hand-wrappings, like other pieces of equipment mentioned here, are available at most sporting goods stores. You can find them easily at stores specializing in boxing and weightlifting equipment. The job of hand-wrapping is an important one that will be explained in Chapter 6.

Skip ropes often are provided by boxing centers, but it is a good idea to have your own. Skipping rope is one method of training that is easily performed away from the boxing center. If

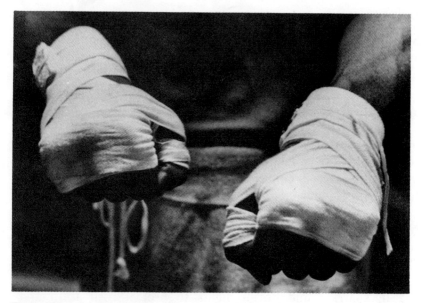

These hand-wrappings protect your hands from injuries in training or in a bout. In chapter 6 you will learn more about these
wrappings. Wrappings are not normally provided by your boxing
club or class, and you will need to purchase your own.

you have your own, you can skip rope wherever and whenever
the opportunity presents itself. You will also find that there
sometimes are not enough skip ropes available at the training
center. If you bring your own along, you won't have to delay
your training routine by waiting for another boxer to finish his
skipping.

Outlook

As important as anything else during your preparation period is
the outlook you have on boxing. If you are committed to
working hard and taking the setbacks as well as the improve-
ments, then you can become a capable fighter.

Some believe that boxing must be a total commitment at all
times, but this is not true. You can succeed in boxing on many

different levels. Just learning the fundamentals of the sport is fascinating, and will get you into very good shape. This takes just a little more commitment than you might give to racquetball, basketball, or any other sport you learn.

To become an amateur fighter of even modest stature you must set your goal at that level and work hard enough to get into matches and do well. Aiming at this goal is more of a commitment.

To become a topflight boxer and possibly have a chance at a professional career, you must make a total commitment from the beginning and use all the ability and intelligence you can muster. Few boxers ever reach this level in the boxing world, but if you believe you have the talent and drive to do it, then push ahead from the beginning.

Set realistic goals when you begin boxing and gear your efforts toward those goals. You can enjoy boxing, no matter which of the above levels you attempt to reach.

2

Getting into Shape

Tom Brookshier, former all-pro defensive back in the National Football League and a CBS boxing announcer, calls boxers the best conditioned athletes in the world. "I'm convinced that boxing takes more out of you than any other sport. I have tremendous respect for the conditioning of boxers," Brookshier has said.

Brookshier hit on one of the most important challenges a potential boxer faces as he contemplates learning to box. You can handle some other sports at less than top physical condition and get away with it, but you cannot even begin to become a good boxer until you are in good shape.

Like many others, when I began boxing instruction I thought I was in good shape. And I was in good shape for some sports, but not for boxing. If this seems overstated, then get up and jump around on your toes for three minutes. If you are an athlete and are only somewhat tired after this exercise, consider those three minutes (the length of a round) of activity combined

Starting your boxing training already in good shape will be
a real plus. Some fighters, like the superbly conditioned
Ken Norton, stay in good shape all year, not just when
training for fights. Your pre-boxing training program will
afford you the same advantage that Norton has when he
begins serious training for a fight. The foundation is there;
he has only to build on it.

with throwing punches, getting hit with punches, and perhaps being leaned on by a man your size or larger.

Most of us who compete in sports on a regular basis don't ever want to admit that we might not be physically able to compete in any sport we choose. But, ego aside, unless you are in superb shape, you will benefit from a two- to four-week preparation period before you ever step into a gym for boxing instruction.

There are two main reasons for following a pre-boxing conditioning program before joining a boxing club or class. First, it will keep you from getting discouraged in the early stages of boxing instruction; and second, it will allow you to improve more rapidly in learning the fundamentals.

The beginning period of boxing instruction can be incredibly frustrating for a young boxer. If you are struggling to get into shape as you learn the boxing fundamentals, the frustration of learning boxing skills will be compounded. If you begin instruction in good condition, that early discouragement can be minimal.

Learning the fundamentals of the sport takes stamina and endurance because you must repeat actions over and over again until you execute them properly. If you are in good shape, you will advance more rapidly because you will not tire as easily. Being in good shape from the beginning simply will help you learn faster because you will be able to execute better, and then you can go on to other skills.

A good program to prepare for boxing instruction includes roadwork (running), rope skipping, basic calisthenics, and weight training (if necessary).

Roadwork is an important element in training because endurance is the single most important commodity for a fighter. Roadwork should be done in a sweatsuit, outside if the weather permits, or inside the gym if necessary. Start at a distance you can handle, like a half-mile. Do that for several days and then start working up gradually. If you can get up to a mile or a mile

In your pre-boxing conditioning program, roadwork is very important. It can be tedious and grueling, but it will be valuable in building stamina. When you start your training at a boxing center, roadwork will remain an important part of your training routine.

and a half of running each day in a four-week preparation period, you will have enough endurance to be ready for boxing instruction.

Speed is not terribly important in doing roadwork, but you must be continually moving. Do not stop for a rest; just slow the pace if necessary. Keep your body loose as you run and keep your arms loose by moving them around and by popping imaginary punches. The best time to run is in the early morning, perhaps before you head for school or work. You are freshest then, and as some boxers say jokingly, it also helps you avoid the bother of explaining to curious onlookers why you are punching the air as you run.

Skipping rope is also a good way to gain endurance and prepare yourself to box. Learning to skip rope is not always easy, and one of the advantages of learning before you set foot in a boxing gym is that you won't be embarrassed by someone who skips better. Even former heavyweight champion Floyd Patterson said he felt embarrassed and awkward because he could not skip rope well in his early days. Because of that, he said he avoided doing it. Don't let that happen to you.

Rope-skipping is a tool to help build stamina and agility, and you can use it not only in your pre-boxing conditioning program, but throughout your boxing training as well. It may be difficult to master at first, but after a short time it will be automatic to you.

Toe touches have long been used by boxers as a stretching exercise. This is a good addition to your pre-boxing conditioning program.

One effective way to learn to skip rope is to run in place slowly and then begin to spin the rope as you run. You will want to alternate feet in skipping rather than jumping up with both feet at the same time. Simply by running in place, you will gain that alternating effect. Start slowly, and when you have mastered this, pick up speed.

For the first week you skip rope, do three or four one-minute skipping sessions with a one-minute rest period in between the skipping. After a week, increase the time of skipping to 1½ minutes with the same rest period. By the time you are finishing your pre-boxing conditioning program, you should be skipping five of the 1½ minute sessions with one-minute rest periods.

This is a good stretching exercise to add flexibility to your body. You must be limber and pliable so that you can handle the strange positions you may be forced into in the ring during a match or sparring session.

Strengthening stomach muscles is important to a boxer, and doing sit-ups is still one of the best ways to do it. The more you do, the better. Here Ken Norton does his daily quota of sit-ups. In chapter 6 you'll see some other ways in which boxers strengthen their stomachs.

In boxing, your body must be limber and pliable. You will be forced into strange positions in the ring, and you must be able to move fluidly to attain those positions. The calisthenics you do must be at least partially geared to providing your body with this flexiblity.

If you use weight training in your pre-boxing program, arm curls are acceptable as exercises. They will help provide arm strength and thus punching power. In this exercise you simply raise the bar from your waist up to your chest, keeping your back straight and using your arms to furnish all the power. As in all weightlifting, breathe out as you lift the barbell and inhale as you let it down. You should do three sets (10 repetitions in a set) of this exercise.

The bench press will help you develop upper body strength, which is valuable to a boxer. For this exercise, push the bar straight up from the chest (exhaling as you do) and then return it to just above chest level (inhaling as it comes down). Don't allow the bar to rest on your chest in between repetitions of the exercise. Do three sets of this exercise, with 10 repetitions in each set.

Stretching exercises have always been a staple of boxing calisthenics and should be done at the beginning of your workout to lessen the chances of muscle pulls later during your workout. Simple toe touches—standing and sitting on the floor—are good, as are windmill stretches, rapid alternating touch of the toes, left foot by the right fingertips, right foot by the left fingertips. Any other kind of flexibility exercise you may run across can be used also. The idea is to get the body limber.

Sit-ups are also essential. The more you do, the better. Strengthening the stomach muscles is vitally important to a boxer. In a later chapter, you will see other ways to strengthen the stomach.

Wrist curls should be done with dumbbells. This exercise can be done during your pre-boxing training and afterwards as well. It strengthens the wrist and forearm. Sit in this position and curl the weight using only the wrist.

Push-ups are important because you obviously need arm strength to box. This is one of the time-honored ways of developing arm strength. You can start with the traditional push-up and then add some wrinkles, like doing them on one arm or clapping as you come up.

While weight training has been accepted in virtually every sport as a good means of increasing strength, most boxing trainers still view it with about as much enthusiasm as they would the plague. A key argument they give against it (often persuasively) is that weight training can overdevelop certain muscles (like the shoulder muscles) and prevent free and easy motion for a boxer. Because of this disadvantage, weight training is discouraged by most trainers.

Though I am not in total agreement with that argument, I still would not suggest weight training as a regular part of the boxer's routine. Some, like light-heavyweight contender Ray Elston, have used it effectively, but the jury clearly is still out on the worthwhileness of weight training for boxers.

While weight training may not be effective for boxers as a training tool after they start boxing, it can be used as a quick way to gain strength in preparation for learning how to box. If a young boxer lacks arm strength and upper body development, there is no better or quicker way to attain it than with weights. You can start this in your pre-boxing program. In four weeks, you will see some improvement, and if you keep at weight training for a month or so after you start your boxing training, you will then be in a position to drop it for the other strength developing exercises that all boxers perform.

Body builders concentrate on using small weights with a large number of repetitions for each exercise. They are primarily looking for attractive bodies. Since that is not your goal (it has never gotten points for a fighter in a close fight), you should use heavier weights with fewer repetitions. Try not to use too heavy a weight, first because you may injure yourself, and second because you may develop too much bulk in your muscles. The idea is to strike a balance between the two extremes of heavy and light. You are lifting for power. You should be looking for arm and upper-body strength if you do not have it already. Only do those exercises that help you to attain that goal. Do arm curls, bench presses, and perhaps wrist curls. Avoid any exercises designed for the shoulders or legs. The overdevelopment of the shoulders can be a problem for boxers.

Whatever exercises you choose for this pre-boxing conditioning program, make sure that your workout each day follows a precise routine. You may alternate either exercises or the length of the exercises, or both, but make sure you alternate on some sort of schedule. The more organized and precise your workouts are, the more organized and precise your approach to boxing will be. This kind of approach will carry over to your boxing training and instruction in the gym, as you will see in Chapter 6.

This pre-boxing conditioning program will include many of the exercises you will continue to use when you begin boxing instruction and training in the gym under the watchful eyes of a boxing trainer. In some cases, you will be a step or two ahead, and above all you will be in shape to begin boxing.

In addition to the conditioning program, there are several other kinds of changes in your lifestyle you may want to put into effect before beginning a boxing program. One important change probably will be in your diet. All the working out in the world won't get you ready for boxing if you eat poorly.

There are several time-honored musts for boxers that I heartily endorse. The first is to avoid fried foods if possible, and that really means avoiding junk foods from your favorite carry-out restaurant. The second is to attempt to eat a balanced diet. Many books outline what a balanced diet is, and a trip to your local library will help you find out about that.

Along with new eating habits, most new boxers find they need new sleeping habits as well. Another of those time-honored musts for boxers is that they get plenty of rest. Boxing workouts are strenuous, and you need all the strength and stamina you can muster. Getting the proper amount of rest assures that.

There are some who claim that boxers should allow for a considerable amount of time during the day and evening in which they can simply relax. This is not always practical for boxers who have other commitments, but the idea obviously is to conserve as much energy as possible for training and actual matches. As a beginning boxer you should think about effective ways to do that, within the framework of your own life's schedule.

3
Stance and Movement

Most of us who are athletic have at one time or another thrown a punch or perhaps even blocked one. Thus we have practiced something of the offense and defense of boxing. But even athletes seldom know how to set up properly and move in a boxing ring. Knowing how to do these things is the first lesson a boxer must learn.

The key element to your basic stance in the ring is balance. You want to retain a balanced position in the ring so that a shove or a light blow will not send you down.

There are a number of different kinds of styles used by boxers, but the traditional stand-up (erect) stance still prevails among most amateur and professional boxers. It is the most effective stance for beginners as they learn the fundamentals. Later you may want to switch, but in the beginning, mastering this basic stance will be best.

In this stance, your left foot (for a right-handed boxer, the opposite for a left-handed one) is in front of the right and

This is the basic stance most boxers use in the ring. If you are a beginner, this classic stand-up boxing stance will help you learn the fundamentals. Later you may want to alter this style somewhat.

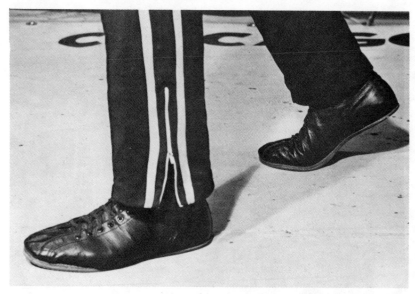

Your feet should be spread apart at a comfortable distance, with your left foot ahead of the right and slightly turned in, if you are a right-handed boxer. Your left foot is flat on the floor, but your right heel is up off the floor.

slightly turned in. The distance between the two feet should be whatever gives you a comfortable and balanced feeling. That feeling depends on variables like your height and the length of your legs.

Your left foot should be flat on the floor, while you keep the heel of your right foot off the floor. Distribute your weight evenly between both feet. Your leg and body weight should not be top-heavy on either the front or back leg. To be sure you are not off-balance in your stance, have someone push you at the shoulders somewhat hard, and see how well you retain your balance.

The upper part of your body should be turned slightly to the left, affording your opponent a smaller target to hit. Some fighters, like heavyweight Ken Norton, accentuate this by turning

Some fighters work better from a crouch. This fighter shows how well you can duck punches and then explode on offense.

far to the left so that part of the back almost shows to the opponent.

Your right hand should be high, reasonably close to your chin, while your left is just below eye level. Always keep your left elbow in close to your body to protect yourself from body blows.

The peek-a-boo style, a variation on the crouch, was made famous by Floyd Patterson. Few fighters have mastered this peculiar style.

Some fighters even move their right hand over to defend and protect their head. Heavyweight Ken Norton uses this style effectively. With the left arm down, a fighter must use the right to protect the head. This more unorthodox style works for Norton and the few other professionals who use it, but beginners might wait before experimenting with this maneuver.

This basic stance is perhaps the only constant for you in the ring. No matter what other positions you are forced into during a fight, return to this one as soon as possible. The reason is simple: You will then be ready to defend yourself or to go on the offensive.

Movement is important for all fighters, and beginning
boxers need to work on fluid movement in the ring. Even
top-notch professionals like Ken Norton have had trouble
with awkwardness in the ring. Norton overcame that
problem with constant work in the gym on his movement.

Some fighters, such as former light-heavyweight champion Archie Moore, have adopted more unorthodox styles. Moore fought out of an extreme crouch. Floyd Patterson also fought out of a crouch, but added a new wrinkle to it called the peek-a-boo style.

This crouch style is frequently effective for shorter fighters. They can duck punches of taller opponents and then explode out of the crouch on offense. Joe Frazier is perhaps the best recent example of a devastating crouch fighter.

One of the traditional axioms in boxing is that you should keep your hands up at all times. That axiom, like others in and out of sports, has been challenged more and more in recent years by successful fighters who do not keep both of their hands up on defense. There are many fighters today who do not keep their left hand up, but find other ways to protect themselves from a right hand by an opponent.

Muhammad Ali is the most notable example, and he in fact pioneered this approach. Boxing experts were appalled when Ali burst on the scene with his left hand dangling at his side, or clenched at his waist. But he was (and still is) effective at avoiding punches by moving, and he uses his left jab effectively by flicking it almost from waist level.

Ken Norton, too, holds his left hand low and has an excellent jab coming up. He protects his head with his right hand crossing over, in a highly unorthodox style. But Norton is considered a brilliant defensive minded heavyweight, so the style has worked for him.

These alterations of the basic stance work for professional fighters after years of experience, but they are not recommended for beginning boxers. Mastering the proper stance will be good enough for now. Any changes you make to fit your style of fighting will come after you have gotten the feel of the ring, and after you have faced opponents of varying styles and ability.

Movement

Your movement in the ring should be as fluid as possible. You want to glide around the ring by sliding the soles of both shoes along.

If you are to move backwards or to the right, then you move the right foot first. If you want to move forward or to the left, then move the left foot first. When you move the lead foot, slide the other one along.

One good exercise to develop proper movement and avoid leg crossing involves moving around in a circle. You slide your feet as you go, first in a circle to the left, and then in a circle to the right. Stop quickly and move back in the opposite direction from time to time. Make sure you lead with the proper foot as you move. You can also use this exercise to develop faking one way or the other. You can fake moving left and go right, or the other way around.

Don't ever get caught *completely* flat-footed in the ring. Your movement from a flat-footed stance is difficult at best. Always keep at least one heel up while gliding, so that you can pivot away at the appropriate time.

Keep your body loose and limber while moving about the ring. If you are tight, you will not move as quickly and you will tire more easily. Don't be alarmed if you are stiff and tight the first few times you actually spar (simulate fighting). Most boxers react that way. Your legs will feel tense and get tired. After a few sparring sessions, you will loosen up more.

Not everyone can move gracefully and smoothly in the ring, and many successful fighters have been plodders. But even the good plodders know how to move in the correct fashion. They simply move a little slower.

If your style is to dance and jab, then you will have to work hard at staying on your toes and moving quickly, as did Sugar

Ray Robinson and other famous boxers of the past and present. If you feel that your punching power is not of the knockout kind, then you will have to work hard on movement so that you can stick and move. Many fighters, such as former middleweight champion Joey Archer, have fashioned entire careers on their ability to stick (throw a punch) and move well.

If you are a knockout puncher and not terribly quick, movement is still important, because you will be chasing fancy boxers. Try to increase your agility with rope skipping and some of the other exercises I suggested in this chapter. Remember that even knockout punchers need to move away from trouble sometimes. If your ability is good and your movement fluid, you'll be able to move away from trouble much easier.

Both the fancy boxer and the slugger need to find their own kinds of rhythm of movement for the ring. In the beginning period of learning boxing, you will be searching for that rhythm. The quest for that rhythm can be difficult and frustrating, but when you are comfortable with your movement in the ring, your confidence and ability will grow immeasurably.

4

Offense

There's an old adage in sports that says you can't win without a good defense. But in boxing, there is no way you can win without a good offense. Some boxers, such as the first black heavyweight champion, Jack Johnson, have been considered defensive geniuses, and no doubt their defensive skills helped them win. But no boxer can win a fight on defense alone. To win a fight, you must either knock out your opponent or outpoint him. In short, you must be able to punch.

Nothing is more important to a boxer than mastering the fundamental punches. And the more of them you master, the better boxer you will be. The greatest fighters, of course, have mastered all the punches, even if they throw some punches better than others. Although some successful fighters have used one punch as their chief weapon throughout their careers, it is generally true that mastering only one punch will not take anyone as far as mastering a number of punches. Former heavyweight champion Joe Frazier, for example, boasted one of the best left hooks in boxing history; and it carried him to the heavyweight crown. But many boxing experts believe that a better right hand—used in conjunction with his left hook—might have enabled Frazier to beat George Foreman and regain his title from Muhammad Ali.

All punches explained in this chapter should be practiced at home or at your training center when shadow boxing (boxing with an imaginary opponent) or when working on the heavy bag. Another good way to practice your punches is in front of a mirror, an action that allows you to see possible flaws in the way you deliver the punches. Practice each punch separately until the movements are automatic to you: then go on to another one.

Here are the basic punches around which you can build an effective attack.

The Jab

For most fighters the jab is the beginning point of their attack. An effective jab can score points, keep an opponent off-balance, and even set him up for other punches.

To learn the jab, stand in your basic stance and extend your arm straight out from the shoulder without making a fist. When you reach what would be the point of impact, rotate your hand to the right. Repeat that motion several times very slowly. Keep your arm slightly loose, not totally limber but not tense either.

After you have made that motion several times, clench your fist, and repeat those motions, this time stepping into the punch by taking a short step with your left foot as you punch. Bring your arm quickly back to the beginning position to protect your face.

Take that short step with your left foot while learning the jab, though you will not always do it in a fight. When you take the step, lift your right heel to give you balance. Don't let your back foot remain flat-footed. As we stated in Chapter 3, you should always try to avoid standing flat-footed.

Starting from the basic stance (left), you deliver the left jab by extending the left arm straight from the shoulder and twisting your glove at the point of impact.

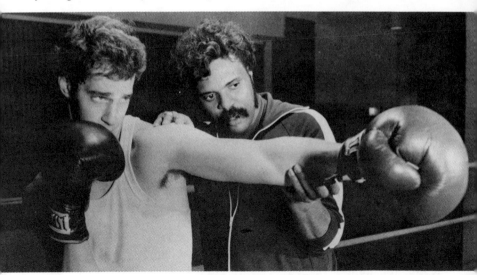

Your coach may spend a lot of time helping you work on your jab, because for most fighters it is the beginning point of their attack.

The right cross involves complete body coordination. You step forward with your left foot and shift your weight from your right leg to your left leg as you deliver the punch. Remember to twist at the waist while you deliver the punch.

Don't try to pick up speed on your jab right away. Though it looks easy, learning to throw a jab quickly in great repetition is a skill that eludes even good professional boxers. Always bring your arm back far enough to gain leverage to throw another jab. Start slowly and build speed over a period of days and even weeks.

Most punches start off the jab; so work hard on this punch. Watch the fighters who are well-known for their jab. Note that no matter how quickly they throw the punch, they follow through each time and concentrate on how and where they are throwing it.

Muhammad Ali may be the best known and perhaps most proficient jabber because of his hand speed, but others, such as Ken Norton and former WBA heavyweight champion Ernie Terrell, have developed jabs almost as good as Ali's.

If you are a heavyweight, then a good jab will be a bonus because big men seldom develop good quick jabs. If you are in a smaller weight division, you will have to become proficient as a jabber to stay with the competition, where the jab is more of a weapon than in the bigger weight divisions.

Right Cross

The right cross is delivered from the basic boxing stance with the right hand up high at shoulder level. Turn at the waist as you deliver this punch, stepping forward with your left foot and shifting your weight from the ball of your right foot to an almost straightened left leg. Your body weight should shift along with the punch so that you can put as much power as possible into the punch. The right cross is frequently a knockout punch for a right-handed boxer.

Probably the most important thing to remember is to turn your body to the left at the waist as you throw this punch. The difference between a potent right cross and a weak one lies in twisting properly and shifting your weight and power into the punch.

When you throw the right cross, remember also to keep your left up high. Many fighters drop their left when throwing a right cross, and they pay dearly for it.

The right cross is usually the second half of the classic one-two combination of punches, which we'll discuss later in this chapter. But the right cross can also be used effectively as a lead punch. Because most action is initiated off the left jab, throwing a lead right cross can be a good tactic if it is used sparingly.

One of the keys to delivering an effective right cross is to turn at the waist to the left as you deliver the punch. You must also remember to shift your weight from the ball of your right foot to your left leg as you throw the punch.

Perhaps the best proponent of this maneuver is Ali. His jab is so good that opponents are looking for it as the beginning of Ali's offense, and he surprises them with a quick, flashing right. His opponents remember the old axiom: "Never lead with your right," and when Ali does it, it is unexpected.

Left Hook

Perhaps no punch in boxing is surrounded by more mystique than the left hook. It has a special place in boxing history, simply because it can be the most awesome of punches. Who can forget the left hook that Floyd Patterson delivered to Ingemar Johansson in their 1960 return title fight? That blow knocked Johansson unconscious for more than a minute. One of more recent vintage was the left hook Joe Frazier used to put Muhammad Ali on the canvas in their famous 1971 title fight.

The left hook is a difficult punch to deliver, but as evidenced by the two previous examples, it can be the equalizer in any fight.

Even more than with the right cross, delivering the left hook properly depends on how well the whole action is coordinated. Start in the basic position and lean forward and to the left slightly. Keeping your elbow tight to your body, turn your left hip and shoulder to the right as you bring your left around with your fist turned inward toward you. Step forward with your left

(Left) To begin the action of the left hook, lean forward and slightly to the left. (Right) You bring a left hook across your body, keeping your elbow as tight to your body as you can, turning your left hip and shoulder to the right as you deliver the blow. This should be a quick, compact motion.

foot, shifting your weight from your right to left foot. Bring the punch straight across if it is a body blow, or bring it slightly upwards if it is aimed at the head.

The left hook should be delivered in a whipping fashion. It should be delivered in as small an arc as possible. A wide looping left hook is easy to block or avoid and leaves you wide open for a counterpunch from your opponent. Delivered in crisp, quick, compact fashion, the left hook can be a devastating punch.

The Uppercut

Throwing an uppercut has been considered a lost art for some time in boxing circles. For a time not many fighters were making effective use of this punch, but in recent years such fighters as lightweight champion Roberto Duran have used it not only as an effective infighting tool, but also as a knockout punch.

The uppercut is primarily used in infighting because it does not require much room to throw the punch. It is a way to get through your opponent's inside defense without leaving yourself open for a counterpunch.

Throw the punch in an upward motion, but in a short arc. Do not wind up and bring your arm far back to throw this punch. Start from the waist and bring the punch straight up to your opponent's jaw. If you are throwing a right uppercut, concentrate your weight on your right foot, and for the left uppercut, on the left foot.

Combinations

A combination is simply two or more punches strung together in a pattern. The idea is to whip several punches at your opponent without giving him time to respond or defend against them.

As a beginning fighter, you will not be expected to become a

Bring all your weight into the punch when you deliver an uppercut. Use a short backswing and shift your weight to the front foot when throwing this punch.

great combination puncher very soon, but in your training center your coach will probably make you aware of some of the basic combinations. They can be used in sparring sessions almost immediately, and if you can master even one good combination, it will help you a great deal in the ring.

The first combination any fighter learns is the one-two combination, which consists of a jab followed quickly by a right cross. Timing is important here. You stick the jab and as you bring your left arm back, immediately fire a right cross. The action should be a quick one-two motion.

Muhammad Ali has been a master of this combination as was Sugar Ray Robinson. Both of these fighters have incredible hand speed, and that helps in delivering any combination.

You build on each combination to create the next one. A natural follow-up to the one-two is to add another punch to it. You can easily add a left hook onto the end of the one-two. After you have thrown the right cross, continue by whipping a left hook as you bring your right hand back to defend. Some trainers believe it is a good idea to crouch slightly when you follow the right with a left hook.

Many combinations can be taught, but the key thing to remember is that they all come from the basic punches outlined in this chapter. As you mature as a fighter, you will see more possibilities for combinations than even your coach may teach you. As you are fighting or sparring, if you are a creative fighter, combinations will simply flow. Just use the fundamental punches and work them in combination.

5

Defense

Learning defensive skills may be the most difficult thing facing a new boxer. On offense, you are initiating the action and you know what you will do next, but on defense you are reacting to your opponent's movement. Becoming a good defensive fighter takes good reaction, quick thinking, and good instincts.

Part of the problem may be that we seldom recognize defensive excellence in boxing. Even boxing experts frequently don't give enough credit to boxers who have mastered defensive skills. And to compound the matter, judges at ringside often don't differentiate between blocked or slipped punches (those a fighter moves aside from) and those that have landed and scored points.

But despite these injustices, the good defensive fighter reaps his own rewards because he will not be hurt so often and will be around at the finish of most fights with at least a chance for victory.

The first commandment of good defense has more to do with

offense. You must never enter a fight believing that you will rely only on your defense for a few rounds or more. Even if you have a plan that involves less activity on offense during some rounds, never forget to provide some offense. The key to any good defense is to keep your opponent at least somewhat concerned about your offense.

In your early sparring sessions you may be reluctant to throw punches, and you will be given a graphic example of how that can cost you. Even at that stage, you may be able to block some

Slipping punches is an important part of defensive boxing. Here a fighter slips a right cross and is in a position to counterpunch.

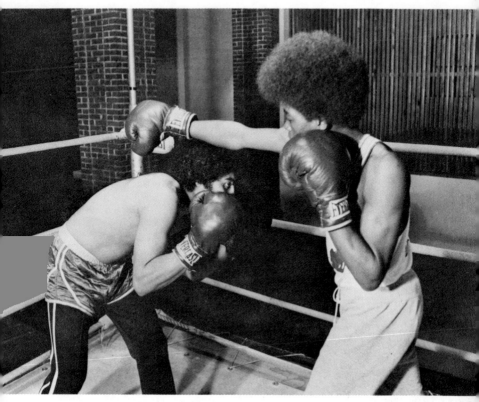

Ducking a flurry of punches is also a very effective defensive ploy. Crouch fighters frequently duck punches.

punches and slip some others, but unless you are answering back with an offense of your own, you will be a sitting duck.

There are really only two options open to you in stopping punches by your opponent. You can slip the punch or block it. Both methods are acceptable, and depending on your situation in the ring, either may be more useful than the other at a particular time.

Slipping punches is more difficult than it appears. You can slip a punch in either direction, of course, and there is considerable

You can "pick off" a punch like the left jab by pushing it away with the right glove.

debate as to whether it is better to slip it on the inside or the outside line. On the inside you would be slipping a right hand by moving to the right, and on the outside by moving to the left. On the inside line you will be able to counter better, but you may be more vulnerable to actually getting hit by the blow. On the outside you are more likely to avoid the blow, but you will probably not be in good position to counter. I believe you should go in whichever direction is easier for you at the time.

Slipping punches also can mean leaning back to avoid a blow. Few boxers are capable of doing this well without either getting tagged with a punch, or getting off balance enough to ruin their tempo in the ring. Muhammad Ali is the best at this and even some young boxers such as Olympic gold medal-winner Howard Davis have adopted this style with some effectiveness. For the beginning boxer, leaning back can be a dangerous maneuver.

(Left) To block a left hook to the body, you must have your right arm in close to your body, with your right forearm and elbow protecting your side. (Right) To block a left hook to the head, you must slide your right arm slightly up and use the glove or arm to catch the blow.

An effective way to block a right cross is with a sweeping motion of your left arm. You push the punch to the outside, as this drawing shows.

Slipping punches in whatever fashion possible is generally good because you have both your hands free to counterpunch your opponent. The danger is obvious; if you miscalculate and don't slip the punch entirely, you have no defense.

Blocking a punch provides more protection, but leaves you only one hand with which to counterpunch.

The first rule for blocking punches is to use only one hand. Many beginning boxers (I was guilty of this) put both hands up to block a blow. This is bad for two reasons; first, because you will leave some part of your body unprotected with both hands up; and second, because you will not have a hand free to counterpunch. Your opponent is a cinch to get in another blow before you can reset yourself and deliver a punch.

Good defensive fighters are able to tie up their opponents when in a clinch. To do it, you pin his arms to his body as best you can— until the referee breaks you.

One term used for blocking a punch is "picking it off." If your opponent throws a left jab, for instance, you would probably use your right to pick it off. You could leave your glove open and practically catch it and push it away, or simply brush it to the side. When you pick off a punch in this manner you always shove it to the outside so that you can counter inside the punch.

Blocking a left hook is a different kind of action than blocking a jab. You keep your right arm in close to your body, and if the punch is delivered to the body, you block it with your arm or elbow. If the punch is directed at your head, then you move your arm up and use the glove to catch the blow. You will find it important to keep your right in this position as a protection, because hooks to the body can be devastating blows.

To block the straight right cross or any variation of the right cross, use your left arm in a sweeping motion, pushing the punch to the outside if you can. The right cross is a good punch to slip whenever possible. If you do block it to the outside, however, you will be able to counter with your own right and then follow up with a left sometimes before your opponent can set himself again.

There are many parts that make up the whole of defensive boxing, and one involves actually stopping punches before they can be thrown. You will find yourself in clinches frequently and (especially if you are in some trouble) you should try to tie up your opponent. Tying him up simply means using whatever means are necessary (and legal) to make your opponent inoperable while you do your own infighting. It is not easy to tie an opponent up, but if you can prevent him from doing damage inside, you will be doing a good job defensively. If you do tie him up for more than a few moments, the referee will break you from one another.

There are different kinds of defensive maneuvers, ranging from the "peek-a-boo" style of Floyd Patterson that I have mentioned to the highly unorthodox "rope-a-dope" style that Muhammad Ali used against George Foreman in their title fight in Zaire. Ali's tactic of covering himself up and leaning against the ropes until Foreman punched himself out worked well for Ali, but this maneuver is not recommended for beginners. Even professionals find that hard to pull off. Evidence of that is the fate Joe Frazier met when he tried the same tactic against Foreman a year or so later. Foreman knocked Frazier out in the fifth round.

You may find new and different ways to protect yourself that are not mentioned here, and obviously they are acceptable if they work for you. Archie Moore from time to time used what some called his "armadillo" style defense. When an opponent started a flurry, he wrapped his arms around his head with both elbows pointing out. If it looked like Moore was taking punishment, he was not. The blows were landing on his arms and gloves. Heavyweight Ken Norton has adopted that same defense on many occasions and uses it well.

Norton is a good example of a fighter who works on defense and uses a number of different maneuvers, including the "armadillo" defense. He is very adept at picking off punches, and is perhaps the only man able to match the quick hand speed of Muhammad Ali by picking off Ali's punches frequently in their fights with each other. A young fighter can use Norton's genius for defense as an example of what good defensive boxing can do for you. If some of Norton's methods are beyond you now, his effort in this area serves as a good model of what defense can do for a fighter.

If you use the classic stand-up boxing style recommended here for beginners, a key will be to keep your hands up. If you don't, you'll learn a painful lesson in your early sparring sessions. It is not easy to keep your hands up, especially as a bout wears on and you become arm-weary. Just taking punches on the arms can be fatiguing. But during training you must constantly be thinking about keeping your arms up.

Much of what you do on defense in the ring will depend on your basic instincts of protection. But if you can learn the proper ways to react defensively and practice blocking and slipping punches correctly in training, then you will improve on defense. A good exercise is to have a fellow boxer shoot punches (light ones) at you and to practice certain kinds of defensive responses. Tell him to mix up his combinations and then defend against them as well as you can. Also isolate certain individual punches you have a hard time stopping and work on those over and over again. If you do this at each training session, in addition to your sparring, your responses to certain punches will become automatic. Then in a match that instinct for protection will include the proper defensive moves.

6

Training

The amount of time a boxer actually spends in matches is tiny compared to the time he spends in the gym training to get ready for those matches. Even a busy amateur who may fight 20 bouts a year will be in the ring only a total of about three hours for the year. That fighter will have spent hundreds of hours in the gym preparing for those fights.

With that as background, it is no wonder that many boxing trainers believe that most fights are won and lost in the gym as fighters train for the fight. Training is the very essence of boxing, and good fighters are fighters who train well.

A good training session should have a tempo and rhythm of its own, just like a fight. It should be organized but not monotonous, and it should be serious but not grim. It should also be something you come to enjoy, if not for the work you do, then for the benefits you know will result from it.

A good training session generally starts with some running, even if you have done roadwork earlier in the day. The running and 15 to 30 minutes of calisthenic type exercises get you ready for the rest of the workout.

Before you do any boxing training, however, you must have your hands wrapped. This hand-wrap (mentioned in Chapter 1) will help prevent injuries to your hands. Your hands always must be wrapped before sparring, hitting the heavy and light bags, and of course, before fighting any bout.

The actual wrapping may be done by a trainer before a fight, but in training you will likely be called upon to do your own wrapping. It will take a few weeks to learn this skill thoroughly, but stick with it and learn to wrap as well as you can. You may be preventing your own injury.

The key to hand-wrapping is to wrap as tightly as you can without cutting off the circulation to the hand. The tighter the wrapping, the less chance you have of suffering a hand injury.

You also want to pay particular attention to covering your wrist. Good strong wrapping there is essential to prevent a broken wrist. Never spar or punch the bag if you think your wrappings are not done well. Ask a trainer for help.

After the calisthenics, your coach at the boxing club or class may have any number of ways of organizing the rest of the workout, but you should take note of whether he *is* organizing it. The more dead time during which boxers stand around, the more haphazard the workout becomes and the more haphazard their approach to boxing becomes. Planned rest time is one

It is important that you have your hands wrapped properly before training in a gym. The sequence of photos on pages 55 and 56 illustrates the general way a coach wraps a young boxer's hand. The main points are to protect the wrist as much as possible, to cover as much area on the hand as you can, and to wrap as tightly as you can without cutting off circulation to the hand. After a few tries (with a coach's help) you should be able to handle this. If you are ever unsure of the wrapping job you have done, ask your coach to look at it. Don't ever train or spar with hand wrappings that are not properly done.

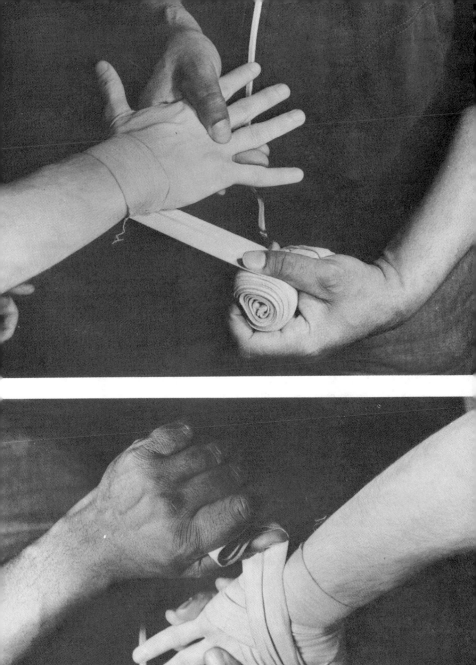
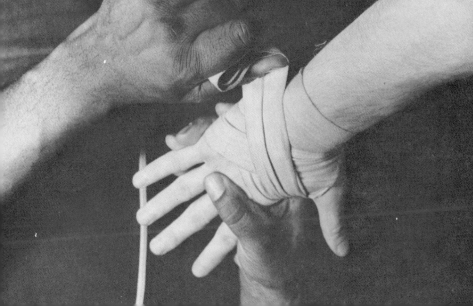

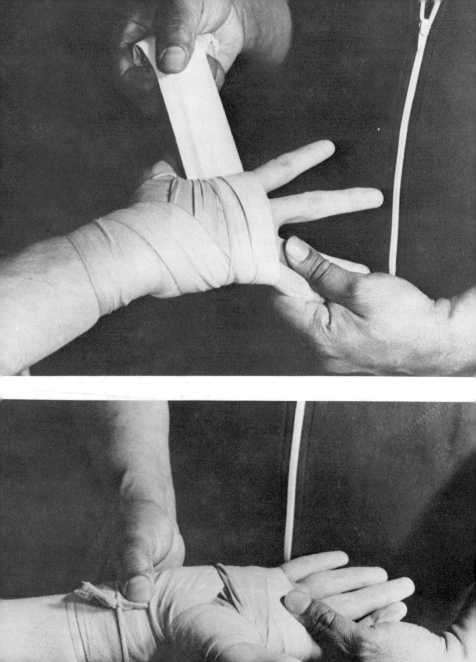

thing, but dead time for no particular reason is not acceptable in a good boxing workout.

It is likely that during the workout, you will interchange your efforts among shadow boxing and working with the speed bag, the medicine ball, and the heavy bag.

Shadow boxing appears, on the surface, to be the most aimless of exercises for fighters, in which they shoot out practice punches to loosen up. Such is not the case. When you shadow box you are practicing punches so that you will throw them correctly in a fight or in sparring sessions. When shadow boxing you should always throw out punches with thought-out combinations, and concentrate on how you are throwing them.

Generally a coach will watch you as you shadow box. One good exercise which is frequently used involves a coach calling out punches he wants you to throw as you move around shadow boxing. He may also call out the direction he wants you to move in.

A fighter asked me once during a training session, "How's your stomach, pretty strong?" I said yes, it was pretty strong. After all, I was doing more than 100 sit-ups a day in training, along with leg raises and other stomach-strengthening exercises. He only smiled and said, "OK, let's see."

That's when I was introduced to the medicine ball. This large heavy ball first got major exposure when Sonny Liston was seen on television getting a medicine ball bounced off his stomach as part of his training for his second fight with Floyd Patterson.

My fellow boxer instructed me to stand about five feet away from him. He then said he would throw the ball to me and I would catch it by tensing my stomach muscles and letting it hit the stomach before catching the ball. He threw it, it hit, I caught it, and I realized that what I had really just received was the equivalent of a body shot from another fighter. It hurt enough to tell me that I needed more than sit-ups to strengthen my stomach for boxing.

That exercise of tossing the ball into the stomach is a good

Shadow boxing is much more than the loosening-up exercise
that some people believe it is. Boxers use their shadow boxing
sessions as a means to practice delivering punches in the proper
fashion. Here Ken Norton uses a mirror during shadow boxing to
tell him if he is delivering punches correctly.

Boxers use the medicine ball in training to build up resistance to body blows. Here Ken Norton catches the medicine ball in the stomach, absorbing the total impact on the stomach.

Another good use of the medicine ball in training is shown in this exercise. One boxer stands over another and drops the medicine ball (from a short distance) onto the fighter's stomach. The ball should be dropped at least 10 times. when this is being done to you, keep your stomach stiff and breathe out through your nose as the ball makes contact.

one, and there are several others involving the medicine ball. In one, a boxer lies down while another boxer or the trainer drops the ball on his stomach and sides in quick repetitions from a foot or so above. The fighter on the ground should breathe out through his nose as the ball hits each time. About a minute of this a few times during a workout will help you get ready for the body blows you will absorb during a fight.

Another good exercise with the ball involves putting it on the mat and rolling over it with the pressure on your stomach. Then you can push yourself up and land on the ball with your stomach. About ten of these exercises generally top off your work with the medicine ball in each training session.

Developing hand speed is the goal of every fighter, and one of the best ways to do it is by working on the speed bag. It takes only a session or two to get the timing of the bag down. Go slower at the beginning to get the rhythm, and then after a few sessions, you'll be making the bag beat a quick tune.

To firm up the midsection, boxers roll on the medicine ball; they also push up and drop down on it a number of times.

Work on the speed bag is also important for arm development, and many fighters simply enjoy the almost hypnotic rhythm of the bag. When you work the bag, keep your hands up at all times. Doing this works as good training for keeping your hands up in the ring.

While your work on the speed bag is primarily for hand speed, the work you do on the heavy bag is for power. Work on the heavy bag is the closest you can come to hitting a person without actually doing it. If you feel you do not have enough power in your punch, then the heavy bag is the most likely place to find that power.

Many fighters have made the heavy bag a key to their training for specific fights because they felt they needed more power for an opponent. For the beginning boxer, work on the heavy bag is a must.

Generally, coaches have you work on the heavy bag in intervals of anywhere from one to three minutes with rests in between. The coach will often call out punches or combinations and urge you to work them to different parts of the bag. You can simulate head or body shots by working to different parts of the bag. This work, like shadow boxing, should be done with thought and purpose, not just aimlessly.

When you are working alone on the heavy bag, practice your combinations and your infighting. Working in close to the bag, rip your shots and practice covering up to defend yourself. Think of the bag as a man who is leaning on you.

To build stamina, sometimes coaches have boxers stand at the bag and punch in bursts for three minutes straight (a round) without stopping or moving. When you can handle this work

Ken Norton's hand speed has allowed him to match jabs with Muhammad Ali in their fights. He gained some of that speed and quickness by working on the speed bag, as he is shown doing here. The speed bag is quite beneficial to beginning boxers.

A powerful heavyweight like Ken Norton gains much of his pu
ing power from work on the heavy bag. Here Ken works on hi
hook. Beginning fighters should work especially hard on the h
bag, practicing combinations and attempting to gain pun
power.

Some fighters work in close to the heavy bag, letting it swing back and forth and pretending it is an opposition fighter.

effectively for three times with one minute intervals of rest, then you will be ready for your first bout in terms of punching stamina.

There is one more element to a good training session, and that, of course, is sparring. You may not spar in each session, but your coach should give you enough work in the ring to get you ready for a match.

Some fighters believe that sparring must be a war at all times, and that may be where the phrase "leaving your fight in the gym" came from. Some fighters, like Sonny Liston before his second fight with Muhammad Ali, have indeed turned their sparring sessions into complete war, and then have been drained for the real fight. Sparring sessions are not matches; they are meant for learning and perfecting skills.

As a beginner, your first sparring sessions are important psychologically. First, you should be wearing protective headgear when you spar, and the two fighters should be using training gloves. These gloves are more spongy than regular boxing gloves. They are generally 16 ounce gloves.

In your first sessions of sparring, you should not be in against a fighter who is far superior to you, unless that fighter understands that this is a learning session and can handle the awkwardness of a beginner. A sparring session against a better fighter who simply wants to beat on you could be a damaging blow to your spirits.

In sparring sessions, you want to practice the punches and combinations you are learning, as well as the defense it takes to stop them. The punching need not be hard in the first few sessions, and sometimes coaches even have you walk through many of the motions with each other.

When sparring sessions do get down to some reasonably heavy hitting, you will have to deal with the major boxing intangible—fear. You will discover in those sparring sessions whether you have the fortitude it takes to give and accept punishment in the ring. Be advised that those first serious sparring sessions will not be easy. You will not be used to breathing with your mouthpiece in place, so you may be short of breath. Your legs probably will be stiff and a bit pained. And after you have been hit with a few good shots, you may wish that you were playing basketball. But if you string together a good combination or block a punch or two, your confidence and relish for the task at hand may grow. Don't let one or two sparring sessions dictate whether you continue with boxing. Give it a reasonable chance. If you are in good shape and learn the fundamentals, you soon will be able to hold your own.

Sparring is an important part of any training session. Sparring sessions should not be total wars, but rather learning sessions for both fighters involved. Note that these two fighters are wearing protective headgear as they spar. If your early sparring sessions are not totally successful, don't let it discourage you. Few fighters do well in initial sparring sessions. Give yourself some time to improve.

As an amateur fighter, you will, in effect, always be training for a fight. Professionals set up special training camps and condense training into a period of a month or two. You will probably train less intensely over the whole year. As a result, you must train hard near a tournament time or when you are gearing up for a series of fights, and then give yourself a little rest when there are not any fights on the near horizon. Only you know how you feel, and you and your trainer should try to suit your training habits to your capabilities.

7

Ring Generalship

In boxing, perhaps more than in any other sport, it is difficult to make the transition from mapping out strategy to actually executing it. Accomplishing that goal and learning to adjust to new developments in the ring are the elements that go into what I call ring generalship.

Becoming a ring general is not something you'll shoot for in your first few months of boxing. Some boxers never attain that status. But you should remember that boxing is not composed of simply getting in the ring and brawling your way to victory. The strategies are sometimes complex and always important.

To be a good boxer you must be able to think in the ring. At the beginning, you may be too frightened or nervous to think clearly when you are sparring or even by the time you have your first bout, but you should try anyway.

One experienced boxer told me when I was first training: "All the things you learn now will fly out the window in your first match and you will be flailing away and slugging it out. You

Ken Norton is one of the few fighters to achieve the status of ring general. Norton, like other ring generals, has the ability to control situations in the ring, rather than letting them control him. Becoming a good ring tactician like Norton takes time and effort.

won't think about what you're doing. It always happens that way. After a match or two, you'll settle down."

That bit of unwelcome analysis is accurate for virtually all young boxers. Even if you take this chapter on boxing strategy as literally as you can, you still will not be able to become a ring general in your beginning period. But you will be able to lay the foundation.

First, you must forget the old myth that only artistic boxers are ring generals. You need not be a Sugar Ray Robinson or Muhammad Ali to earn that status.

An important part of becoming a ring general is to take stock of your assets as a fighter. Do this honestly because you may be able to fool yourself, but you will not fool your future opponents.

Evaluate yourself using the kinds of traditional guidelines people have always used to rate fighters. Assess your own foot and hand speed, punching power, physical dimensions, stamina, and courage.

After you have located your strengths, then begin to build a style that takes advantage of those strengths and minimizes any weaknesses you may have. If, for instance, you are short and stocky with good punching power and good stamina, a crouch style might be appropriate. Joe Frazier fought from this crouch style, using it to get inside his opponent's reach. Once inside, he used his shorter arms and punching power to do damage. From outside they would be ineffective.

To work on this style you need to practice bobbing and weaving and to learn the art of infighting. Learning these skills will occupy much of your training, especially in the beginning period.

If you are tall, quick, and have a long reach, the classic stand-up style of boxing might be more suitable. Here you could use reach and quickness to your advantage.

In many cases, your style will be dictated by the sparring sessions in which you find out more about those things you can

Sparring sessions can be used as part of the process of evaluating yourself as a fighter. These sparring sessions will demonstrate some of your strengths and weaknesses. Use this knowledge to develop a style that takes advantage of your strengths and minimizes your weaknesses.

and can't do in the ring. In any case, your evaluation process should be an ongoing thing.

Finally, you must develop your strategy for each fight (and each sparring session for that matter) based partially on your opponent's strengths and weaknesses. Spotting these is not always easy, especially for a beginning boxer. To improve your ability to spot strengths and weaknesses, watch other boxers as they work in the gym in sparring sessions, and watch as many amateur and professional fights as possible. You should study them all with a critical eye toward all the varied styles boxers present.

Each fight for a boxer represents a new challenge, and sometimes you will be forced to come up with a slightly different approach. There is a long-standing debate as to whether boxers should change their style for specific fights. The real answer to that debate is that no matter how hard they try, fighters seldom really change their style after they have developed one that suits them. They simply add and subtract things to give the appearance of a new look.

There are several standard ways of changing the appearance of your style to confuse an opponent. One is to add a punch you have not thrown before, or to change the way you throw it.

One good example was in the 1976 fight between Muhammad Ali and Ken Norton. Norton, who had fought Ali twice before, losing once and winning once, found that he could not get a straight right hand through the Ali defense. So, in training before the 1976 fight, Norton worked on a looping overhand right that came over the Ali defense. The move befuddled Ali, and despite the awkward appearance of the maneuver, it scored heavily for Norton throughout the fight, and nearly won him a close decision.

Another apparent style change is to start a fight or a specific round by doing something that is totally uncharacteristic of you as a fighter. For instance, if you are a slugger known for your straight-ahead style, you may spend part of a round laying back and luring your opponent in where you can unload. As elementary as this sounds, many sluggers have used this maneuver and have found curious opponents who fell prey to the trick. Counterpunchers like heavyweight Jerry Quarry have used this maneuver effectively.

The key to these maneuvers is to use them sparingly and not let them interfere with the style and tempo of fighting that you have worked so hard for hundreds of hours in the gym to perfect.

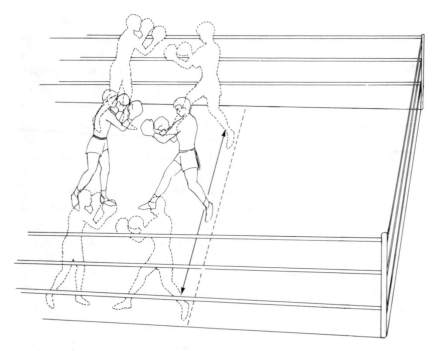

An important maneuver for a slugger in against a fancy boxer is to cut the ring in half. Here we see how a fighter does this by moving from side to side, cutting off the escape route to the other half of the ring. Here the boxer on the right has cut off the ring.

Frequently when a fighter totally changes his style for a fight, the results can be disastrous. Once you have developed a style that works for you, don't allow an opponent to dictate the terms of the fight even before the fight has begun by changing your style to suit him. To do so is practically an admission to the opponent that you are not equipped to handle him without some gimmicks.

Depending on your style, there may be many tactics you can use in the ring. You should work on them in your sparring sessions as diligently as you can.

If you are more of a slugger fighting a classic boxer, there are several maneuvers you can use. First you should attempt to cut the ring in half. This is a well-known boxing expression that means exactly what it says. You try to keep your opponent in one half of the ring by cutting off his escape to the other half. The key here is to move from side to side quickly enough to keep him contained and then move in to mix it up.

Another time-tested tactic against a quick boxer is to go to the body often in the early part of the fight so that your opponent will be slowed down in the latter stages of the fight. As the fight wears on, body punches take their toll. Good body shots early in the fight can make a big difference later on.

When you have a boxer against the ropes, be sure to use your body to lean on him and apply pressure. You want to make him know you are there and that there is pressure every moment. That contact and leaning takes a physical and psychological toll in a fight.

For a classic boxer there are just as many tricks you can use when you are in against a brawler or a heavy hitter or a fighter who is both. First you will want to keep your opponent at bay, and there is no better way of doing that than with an active and stinging left jab. This punch will disrupt his momentum and make it difficult for him to get untracked.

You will also benefit if you know which of your opponent's punches is his most lethal. If you do know, it is a good idea to

spend the entire fight backpedaling away from that punch. Muhammad Ali built his entire fight strategy on this maneuver when he fought Sonny Liston for the first time. He constantly moved in a circle away from the awesome left hook of Liston. Ali circled always to the left, never once moving "into" Liston's most potent weapon.

A good boxer also will be able to tie up a slugger on the inside so that the referee will break them, and he can dance away to safety. You must work on this tactic extensively in the gym.

You will find occasion for a number of these tactics, whether you are slugger or boxer, or a little of both. But whatever you use or fail to use in the ring, always have some idea of what you plan to do when you step into a ring, even for a sparring session. And once you go in, be ready to adapt to whatever situation may come up. Don't just go in to "mix it up." A ring general always has a plan, and if that plan fails, he will adapt what he is doing and try a different approach.

For a beginning boxer, just getting over the fear of being hit is sometimes enough of a chore. All fighters, even the most competent professionals, experience fear before a fight. Some use it to their advantage and others simply let it control them and react as mummies in the ring. Having fear is normal and almost mandatory, but you must control it and deal with it in your mind if you are to succeed in boxing.

One of the best ways to deal with fear of an opponent is to land the first solid blows of the fight. Doing this can raise your confidence and may shift some of the fear to your opponent.

Every time you step into the ring, whether it is to spar or to fight in a match, have a plan of attack. Don't ever get into the ring just to "mix it up." Here, in a sparring session, Ken Norton looks to go to the body.

You cannot become a ring general unless you are in control of the situation in the ring, and you will never be in control if your opponent believes you are afraid. Some ring generals mask their fear with antics like Muhammad Ali, others with surliness like Sonny Liston, and still others with apparent workmanlike detachment, like Joe Frazier or Ken Norton. Whatever your method, you must make your opponent know that you do not fear him.

Besides overcoming the fear, ring generalship takes the qualities that all good athletes have: intelligence, a good grasp of the sport, and an organized approach. Just a little of each of those qualities can send you a long way in the sport of boxing.

Glossary

APRON: The part of the ring floor that extends beyond the ropes.

BACKPEDAL: To retreat from an opponent though still facing him.

BARRAGE: A succession of punches by one boxer against another. Usually these are hard and fast punches.

BEAT TO THE PUNCH: To hit your opponent first, although his punch started at the same time, or even before.

BELL: The gong that is used in most places to signal the start and finish of a round.

BELT: The line around the body at the level of the navel. Hitting below the belt is a foul.

BETWEEN ROUNDS: The one-minute interval from the end of one round to the beginning of the next.

BODY BLOW: A punch landed to the body of a fighter.

BOUT: A boxing match.

BRAWLER: A fighter who is not a fancy boxer, but instead uses a very physical approach that includes leaning on his opponent, muscling in, and sometimes even such illegal tactics as butting.

BREAK: The separation of two fighters by the referee when they are clinched together and all action has stopped.

BUTT: To hit an opponent with a head or shoulder. This is a major foul, and repeated use can lead to disqualification.

CLASSIC STANCE: The basic stance taught to most beginners: left foot flat, forward, and slightly turned in, heel of right foot off the floor, upper body turned slightly left, right hand high and close to chin, left just below eye level.

CLINCH: When two fighters have locked arms while fighting in close.

COMBINATION: Throwing two or more punches in rapid succession. The classic one-two combination is the left jab followed by the right cross.

CONTENDER: A fighter who is ranked in the top ten in his weight division and may have a chance to fight for the championship.

COUNTERPUNCH: A punch thrown in response to one thrown by the opponent.

COVERING UP: A defensive maneuver in which a boxer uses both arms to cover the body and head. This tactic is generally used when a fighter is in trouble and needs to last out a short time before the end of a round.

CROUCH STYLE: A fighting style in which the body is bent down and out of which the fighter explodes to go on offense. This style is used frequently by shorter fighters with a shorter reach.

CROWD: To move in close to an opponent in an effort to cut off his punching room and apply your own offensive pressure.

CUTTING THE RING IN HALF: Containing an opponent by allowing him only half the ring to move in. You slide from side to side, not allowing him access to the other side of the ring. Sluggers generally use this tactic against quick and nimble boxers.

DUCKING: Dropping the body down and forward to avoid punches.

FEELING-OUT PROCESS: The initial period of a fight when both fighters appear tentative about unloading heavy punches. They are attempting to learn more about their opponent's style.

FEINT: A false lead to one part of your opponent's body, used to draw him off guard.

FLOOR: To knock an opponent down.

FOUL: To break the rules of boxing.

GETTING UNTRACKED: The process of getting into your rhythm as a fighter. Some fighters never get untracked in a fight and suffer a defeat as a result.

HAND-WRAPPINGS: The bandage-type material you use to wrap your hands before training and a bout.

HEAD-HUNTER: A fighter who disdains working to the body and tries only for a good shot to the head.

HEAVY BAG: A large canvas- or leather-covered bag filled with sand, sawdust, or some other material. This bag is used to develop punching power.

HOOK: A punch delivered at close range from the side, usually a left hook.

INFIGHTING: Fighting at close range.

JAB: A straight punch, delivered from the shoulder. The left jab (for a right hander) and right jab (for a left hander) are the beginning point of most fighters' attacks.

KNOCKDOWN: Flooring an opponent.

KNOCKOUT: A knockdown in which the fighter floored is unable to get up within 10 seconds. This is one way of winning a boxing match.

LOW BLOW: A blow below the belt line. This is a foul.

MEDICINE BALL: A large, heavy ball used to strengthen a fighter's stomach and sides, and to build up resistance to body blows. Boxers catch it in the stomach, roll on it, and have it dropped on them.

MIXING IT UP: A phrase used to denote action in the ring.

MOUTHPIECE: A rubber or plastic protector used as covering for the teeth.

NEUTRAL CORNER: The two corners of the ring not used by the fighters between the rounds. Fighters are instructed to go to one of these corners after knocking down an opponent.

OUTPOINT: To gain the decision of the officials over your opponent without knocking him out. It means that you have hit your opponent more often and more effectively than he has hit you.

PEEK-A-BOO STYLE: A boxing style made famous by Floyd Patterson in which the fighter puts both gloves around the sides of his head and "peeks" out to see his opponent. This is a variation on the crouch style.

PICKING OFF PUNCHES: A term used for blocking punches by catching them on a glove before they land.

RIGHT CROSS: A righthand punch that crosses from right to left. It is delivered with a twist of the waist and upper body to the left.

RING GENERAL: A fighter who has mastered the fundamentals of boxing and has the savvy to control most situations in the ring. This is a fighter with experience and know-how.

ROADWORK: The extensive running a boxer does to gain stamina and endurance.

ROUND: The three-minute period in amateur and professional fights in which the fighters compete. A number of these rounds make up a complete fight. All amateur fights are three rounds, but professional fights go longer. All title fights in the professional ranks are 15 rounds.

SHADOW BOXING: Sparring with an imaginary opponent.

SKIP ROPE: The rope you use to skip with during training to build stamina and endurance.

SLIPPING A PUNCH: To avoid a punch by moving the head or body away from the punch to either side.

SPARRING: Boxing in training that simulates conditions in an actual bout. Fighters wear protective headgear when sparring.

SPARRING PARTNER: A man you spar with during training.

SPEED BAG: A small, lively bag you punch to build up hand speed.

SPEED GLOVES: Gloves used in training for working on the speed bag and the heavy bag.

STAND-UP BOXER: A fighter who fights from the classic stand-up stance.

TECHNICAL KNOCKOUT: When a fight is stopped by the referee because of an injury, or because a fighter in his opinion is taking too much punishment.

TIE-UP: To clinch and lock your opponent's arms against his body so that he can't do damage to you inside.

TRAINING: The conditioning a fighter does leading up to a match.

UPPERCUT: A blow delivered with an upward motion in which all the weight is concentrated on the front foot.

Index